A PINCH OF SALT

A PINCH OF SALT

In the Recipe Called Life

Sanjay K. Jain

BLOOMSBURY
NEW DELHI • LONDON • OXFORD • NEW YORK • SYDNEY

BLOOMSBURY INDIA
Bloomsbury Publishing India Pvt. Ltd
Second Floor, LSC Building No. 4, DDA Complex, Pocket C – 6 & 7,
Vasant Kunj, New Delhi 110070

BLOOMSBURY, BLOOMSBURY INDIA and the Diana logo are trademarks of
Bloomsbury Publishing Plc

First published in India 2020
This edition published in 2020

ISBN:TPB: 978-93-89449-92-1; eBook: 978-93-89449-94-5

2 4 6 8 10 9 7 5 3 1

Typeset by Manipal Technologies Limited
Printed and bound in India by Thomson Press india Ltd.

FSC
www.fsc.org
MIX
Paper from responsible sources
FSC™ C010615

All papers used by Bloomsbury Publishing are natural, recyclable products from wood grown in well managed forests. The manufacturing processes conform to the environmental regulations of the country of origin

To each and every person who has been part of my golden life journey

CONTENTS

PREFACE

It all started one day while I was waiting at the airport; I came upon the subject for my book (an important item on my bucket list). It was at that moment that the idea to web together my experiences, thoughts, ideas and perspectives of different things in life dawned upon me. So, here I am, presenting it before my fellow human beings with a hope that I shall be able to provide some insights and values to them.

I am not going to discuss the topics of each chapter. Instead, I prefer all my readers to go to the contents page and scan the different chapter headings. Every chapter is based on a different theme, principle or perspective. However, they are all still knitted, woven and linked together.

For me, life is like a rainbow where all colours are equally important to live a happy and balanced life and be complete. A life rainbow can never be created unless we fill it up with all the seven colours and balance them. Variety is indeed the spice of life as it keeps us excited and motivated.

I have always believed that life is never black or white. It has various shades of grey which can look different from different angles. It is for certain that whatever I say can be debated and disputed—the first chapter dwells on this subject. This book has not been written to prescribe a solution or remedy. The objective is to provoke thoughts so that one can find their own equilibrium.

This book is concise and compact. I am just trying to share my thoughts with you, and in that effort, I want to be honest with our environment by ensuring that paper and ink are used sensibly and to the minimum. It reminds me of my school days when I always kept my answers concise, going against the normal tide of filling sheets and making the answer paper-bulky. I was lucky to still get the examiner's thumbs up. Here I will be awaiting your verdict, as you are the examiner of this book.

The ingredients have been picked from the universe of knowledge and are cooked just a bit differently in my style to serve something which will hopefully stir your mind buds positively and pleasingly. This book is a small talk with my fellow human beings. We know so much, but unfortunately, we do little to transform knowledge into action. Many a times, it's not the big things but the many small things which can make a big difference.

Simplicity and focus are very important in life and this book has been written with this mindset. My deliberations and thoughts are not fancy or high-level but very simple and common, like *salt*.

This book tries to add that little 'common' salt (sense) that can change the taste of (y)our life's recipe. It will just add 1 per cent to your 99 per cent to make your life a 100 per cent. A pinch of salt can change the taste of anything, including our lives.

The chapter headings will sound very business-like and the first impression may be that it's only for working people. However, if we delve deeper, the significance of all the chapters will be as much for other sections of the society and segments of our life. The book is meant for the common masses, irrespective of their field of work or interest or gender. I hope you all read this book with equal interest and find your own relevance.

Please read this book slowly and thoughtfully and hope that this *pinch of salt will change the taste of your life.*

Some may decide to take my thoughts with a 'pinch of salt', which is also perfectly fine, as there is never any perfect truth or principle in life. Hence, in whatever context you read the title of the book, it will still be representative of the contents.

Let's move on to the first chapter to discuss the principle of life which has changed my thought process dramatically and made me a more considerate human being. However, before you start reading the book, words of wisdom from people I value and respect for their life journey have been shared on the next page, from which valuable lessons can be drawn.

I have drawn upon my life experiences and not just my business and working life. Interestingly, this book contains nothing that I learnt at the Indian Institute of Management (IIM); it's all about what I learnt from life after graduating from there.

ACKNOWLEDGEMENTS

I would like to thank my parents, wife, children, sister, in-laws, family, teachers, friends and fellow travellers for their constant support, motivation, guidance and inspiration over my fifty years of life. They all have contributed in their own way to make me what I am today and in realising my dream of writing a book into reality.

I would also like to specifically thank my friends Chandrasekhar Shrimali, Mamta Madhavan and my children, Muskaan and Hardik, who have contributed enormously to the proofreading of the book. My heartfelt gratitude to my wife Jyoti who pushed me to start writing.

Also, a very special thanks to Ruchita Kazaria for motivating and introducing me to our publishers—Bloomsbury.

Finally, I would like to especially thank Mr A.M. Naik, Mr S.P. Oswal, Mr Ashok Mallik, Mrs Shikha Sharma, Mr Motilal Oswal and

Mr Gautam Kumra for sharing their words of wisdom to enrich this book. They are role models for all of us and I am sure their words will add a lot of value to the readers.

WORDS OF WISDOM

I requested a few people from different walks of life, whom I admire, to pen down a few success and motivational mantras of their lives, to add that extra salt to ours. It's brief but very intense and worth a pause and thought before you move on to read the book.

Mr A.M. Naik, Group Chairman, Larsen and Toubro, Padma Vibhushan Awardee

Mr A.M. Naik, Group Chairman of Larsen and Toubro (L&T) and architect of its transformation into a vibrant, value-creating organisation, possesses unabating restlessness and a kind of zest that only a few corporate leaders can match. He can never rest or be content with the status quo. The message he sends out is clear and compelling—raise the bar, accelerate, scale up and go global. Always an entrepreneurial leader, he knows exactly how to add value at every stage of an organisation's operations. The spectacular and sustained rise in L&T's market cap since he took over at the helm speaks for itself. Underlying all this, of course, is an abiding spirit of nationalism. As he says, pointing to the tricolour that is pinned onto his coat, 'It's always nation first.'

Mr S.P. Oswal, Chairman and Managing Director, Vardhman Textiles Ltd & Vardhman Group of Companies, Padma Bhusan Awardee

- *Principle of Integrity:*

  Right from the start of my career, I have always held integrity as very important for a leader. What we say, we must practice and what we say, we must believe. This inspires trust in the organisation as a whole, besides giving all members of the organisation a sense of confidence in the management and their actions.
- *Right Culture in the Organisation:*

  Culture has immense importance in the organisation. Culture reflects the values, beliefs and convictions that guide our actions and behaviour in the organisation. A good culture always influences the members of the organisation and prompts them to act in alignment with the same. There's no doubt that it takes a long time. Culture fosters consistent behaviour amongst the members and gives a sense of predictability.

- *Principle of Talent Management:*
  Every organisation which aspires to grow has to devote good time and resources to human development. We cannot always depend upon getting people from outside. Therefore, a need to develop internal talent is of the greatest importance. It also improves the overall working climate as it gives hope to the people to grow and develop the potential that they possess.
- *Principle of Broad Purpose:*
  Invariably, businesses emphasise too much on making profits. There is no denying the fact that the organisation has to produce a profit, even though it exists with a clear purpose of serving the needs of the customers, fulfilment of the employees

and service to the society in many ways. Therefore, when we operate in the context of our industry, we also have a wider purpose like sustainability, our surroundings in whose proximity we exist. Any new location we go to, we have always taken care of our society around and given it a position of dignity and respect. Similarly, we have to ensure that we give due weightage to the customs and traditions of the society, which people respect, and through our policies and actions, also ensure that there is no conflict with the same.

Mr Ashok Malik, Former Press Secretary to the President of India, Columnist and Writer and Padma Shri Awardee

- Be ambitious, but more than that, be inquisitive and curious. The day your curiosity dies, you may as well retire.
- Treat the long term as a series of short terms. It's good to have a long-term strategy about life, career, investments—

anything, but it is better if you have a series of achievable, short-term and immediate future targets.

- Be confident of your abilities and back your instincts. It may be wrong on occasion, but your instinct and your gut will pay off more often than not.
- Beyond a point, don't bother about what people think. One, what others think doesn't matter. Two, chances are they don't think of you as much as you think they think of you.
- Walk into a work environment hoping to make friends but don't make that your absolute priority. If it comes to that, stop feeling sorry for yourself and be prepared for guerrilla warfare. Learn to fight back.
- Don't believe anyone who tells you money doesn't matter. If you don't respect money, it will not respect you.

Mrs Shikha Sharma, Ex Managing Director and CEO, Axis Bank

- Seize every opportunity to learn.

- Do your best to make change where you can and don't fret about what you can't influence.
- Look back only to learn.
- Don't get caught in the trappings. Be ready to walk away every day.
- Live your principles every moment. You are accountable first to yourself.
- Practice gratitude even in the most difficult times. Counting your blessings releases positive energy.

Mr Motilal Oswal, Chairman and Managing Director, Motilal Oswal Financial Services Ltd

I would just share an acronym called KIT which guides my personal and professional life. K for knowledge, I for Integrity and T for the team. The KIT of these three principles have brought huge personal and professional growth for me. While integrity (values) is permanently a part of me, I spend disproportionate amount of time on the other two, that is, learning (knowledge enhancing) and building a great team besides nurturing my relationships with them.

Mr Gautam Kumra, Managing Partner, India Office, Mckinsey and Company Inc.

- *Have high ambition:* As a leader, you are expected to set a high standard.
- *Lead the way:* Before you preach, practise. That's the only way to bring about change.
- *Take responsibility:* Only you and you alone are responsible for your fate. Take ownership of the choices and be ready to live the outcome.
- *Keep good company:* You become the average of the five people you spend most of your time with. Be careful about the company you keep.
- *Invest in yourself:* Know yourselves, learn what to accept and what to change. Be on a journey of continuous growth and never stop learning.

I

Anekantvaad—Perspectives

To change ourselves effectively,
we first had to change our perceptions.
—Stephen R. Covey

I am right and you are wrong—does this sound familiar? Haven't you felt or said this umpteen times? Hasn't this led to many arguments and fights because both sides have felt they were right and the other person wrong? Did it ever strike you that both could be correct? Have we missed something?

We all feel that we are right and our understanding is perfect. We feel that there can be only one right way and that truth is universal. I also used to feel so, until I read and understood the principle of *Anekantvaad* in Jainism. It's the theory of non-absolutism and the doctrine of multifacetedness of reality. If literally translated, it means 'many perspectives' of the same thing. The more I thought about it, the more I was convinced that there could be more than one right or truth for a thing, concept or matter.

I cannot see any perfect perfection in the world. We normally see an imperfect perfection, which, like a mirage, we consider to be the ultimate truth. We are so busy questioning and doubting others that we forget to do the most important thing—to question ourselves!

Most arguments happen because we fail to see things from the other person's perspective. People argue that some things cannot have multiple perspectives. Hence, the argument on who or what is right or wrong. I am reminded of the story of five blind men and an elephant where each man felt the elephant and described it. One touched the ears and thought it was a fan, the other felt the trunk and thought it was a snake, the third touched the legs and said it was a tree trunk and so on. None of them was right or wrong—the simple reason being that they all saw it from different perspectives or angles and made their own inference.

Taking this argument forward, something as ghastly as murder can have a positive angle when someone is killed unintentionally or for self-defence. Hence, even that cannot be universally considered to be wrong. I can go on and on, giving examples to prove that there can be many correct perspectives for the same thing. However, I hope the point is already understood and appreciated.

Now what? We agree everything isn't black or white—there are overlaps and shades of grey. We agree that there can be different correct perspectives and one doesn't have to be wrong for another one to be right. We can have win-win situations and lose-lose situations. However, the moot point is, how can this help us as human beings? This isn't a philosophy book or class but something to help and impact us positively.

The biggest benefit we can derive from understanding and appreciating this concept is that we will be able to avoid unnecessary arguments and disputes. We shall start appreciating others' points of view and respect people. To understand another person's perspective, it is very important to place oneself in the other person's shoes. We shall be able to understand a matter from multiple viewpoints and come to a more balanced and reasonable perspective.

The other important benefit is that our mind's horizon and thinking power will increase as we will look out at problems, issues and hindrances from multiple angles which will help us find solutions more easily. The additive and multiplicative approaches to life expand and they give an unmatched power of visualisation. They lead to the development of innovative powers which are admitted by all as a very important tool to succeed in this ever-changing and fast-moving world.

I strongly recommend you all to ask yourself, is there another angle or perspective? Am I missing something important? Let me look at it from the other person's angle? If I were in that person's shoes, would my conclusions be the same?

Answers in life come when you have questions; it's a natural complement. Unless we have the right questions, we can never find the right answers. Therefore, please do not fear to ask what you have never thought of. We are not in a classroom where we fear being ridiculed when we ask questions; we are in our own private world where we can ask or question anything as the answers will come from within us. We may fear the outside world but let us be fearless in our own world.

I would like to share a simple experience which would help a marketer particularly. We often visit multi-brand shops which house the best of brands designed and created by the leading designers. However, it is funny that many a times we don't find anything suitable and just walk out empty-handed. Was the merchandise that wrong? But then how is this shop running for years? Are we weird? But again, our clothing sense is considered normal by others. Well, maybe the truth lies elsewhere; it's just a case of multiple tastes and preferences of different human beings. The shops that can attract the majority will do well over those who can't go beyond a small percentage. Of course, another perspective comes into play here. One may argue that famous designers just cater to a very small percentage and are still majorly successful and famous over designers who catch the fancy of the masses. Here, we may again argue that it's the price tag that makes it the choice of a few. But don't we sometimes ask ourselves, 'Does the designer-wear look weird and is it meant for those chosen few?'

Anyway, we can go on and on; every road will lead us to a T-road or roundabout from where there are multiple options to branch out. Different people choose different roads. The shortest route also becomes a bad choice if it is overcrowded or broken and sometimes the longer route is a better choice (I'm sure we all make such choices every day).

By now, some of you who have started thinking or activating their grey cells maybe confused or are finding it difficult to really have one absolute choice or answer or truth—there are just so many ifs and buts. Don't worry. That's life and we should not bother about what we missed out (as we all can't be Einstein) but just understand and appreciate the existence of multiple truths, routes, options and perspectives.

Another simple example which we all see and comment about—what is enjoyment and fun? Some love partying and being social while others enjoy their solitude. There are a few others who love being in their own small group and so on. Everyone normally finds the other's way of enjoyment as weird and sometimes stupid. They feel listening to loud music stirs a headache while others feel that not partying is so boring and is a sign of being old. The biggest excitement of one can be a source of headache for another and yet different people are happy doing different things. For instance, on a beach holiday, while someone enjoys lying on the beach with a book in hand, another one is jumping amidst the waves or doing water sports.

Live with your beliefs and convictions but learn to respect and appreciate those of others. As we say, 'live and let live'. No one is weird or stupid; it is just that their perspective of life is different from yours.

Are you ready to accept that others can be right even if they don't agree with you or you don't with them? Just try it and not by compromising or out of sympathy, but by understanding their perspective and viewpoint.

Just remember this beautiful universe bouquet is created with flowers of different kinds and colours. They have come together and created a marvel.

If we just had red roses in the world, the gardens would never have looked as beautiful and amazing as they do.

The chapters in the book touch upon these facets of life and also prescribe certain modes and practices. Despite being a strong believer in *Anketkantvaad*, I am advocating all to follow certain small but meaningful practices because I sincerely believe in them and feel that the probability of them making your life better and happier is high. It's not important whether you follow them or not but what matters is that you understand and recognise them.

The environment in which we exist plays an important role in conditioning us. Our understanding of issues and facts depends so much on the context. Rarely can anything survive in isolation or vacuum, not even fire has existence without air around it. Hence our understanding and acceptance of anything will depend on the environment in which we exist. This further multiplies the possible perspectives and truths.

Truth is never isolated but is relative to the time and environment. Hence, a change of mind or perspective doesn't necessarily mean that the person is a hypocrite or unstable. We need to understand and appreciate the surroundings of a person and accordingly judge him/her. Everyone has the right to change his viewpoint based on experiences, environment and context—to improve and refine thoughts, and beliefs which should always be encouraged and welcomed.

When a flight gets delayed due to airport congestion, we welcome it if we are engrossed in a movie on the in-flight entertainment system. We wish that it lands after the end of the movie. So, the lesson is loud and clear—everything has another perspective.

I would like to conclude by saying—when a person ignores other angles of a situation or substance, he/she shall never be able to understand the real truth.

2

Disruption Is the New Norm

You have to be burning with an idea, or a problem, or a wrong that you want to right. If you're not passionate enough from the start, you'll never stick it out.

—Steve Jobs

For the last decade or so, we have always been saying that change is the new norm and that change is the only constant. However, as we move to the VUCA (Volatility, Uncertainty, Complexity and Ambiguity) World, the new norm is *disruption.*

Change is no more a choice but a compulsion. Disruption is a choice for us to choose. And for those who still think that they can go on without changing, the ground on which they stand will move ahead, leaving them behind. We may be constant, but the environment around us is changing so fast that we experience change and, unfortunately, it may be a negative one for us. Today, the only choice we have is to choose in which direction to change and move on.

Nowadays, life is like a non-stop treadmill where we need to keep pace to ensure we don't crash out. Moving on isn't a choice but a compulsion. We can, however, manage the speed and incline in which direction to move towards and still meet our goals.

Gears and clutch are integral parts of a car. They were needed to change the pace. However, we are slowly moving to automatic gearless cars where change is seamless. Gears and clutch are slowly getting extinct and in times to come, even drivers may vanish and cars will change pace in response to the environment automatically.

The onward movement has become so fast that it is nothing short of disruption. We need to consistently make changes which cumulatively have an impact amounting to disruption.

Therefore, make 'out-of-the-box thinking' a way of life and dare to dream, think and act. In today's world, if we don't endeavour to think out of the box, the box itself may move, leaving us 'out of the box' in a detrimental way.

Disruption isn't just about large abrupt changes but it also means to make many small changes, resulting in disruption and moving onto a different level of existence.

Many feel that this is just for entrepreneurs, but in this tough world where robots and artificial intelligence are rapidly entering the business domain, it's equally applicable for employees. In the past, years were given for learning computers but now you don't get more than months to change.

In the past, generations lived on one family business but now even one generation cannot be sure! If we see the top companies of today—Apple, Google, Amazon, Alibaba and so on, they were not significant a decade or more back. They not only grew but grew like zombies, leaving the best of the best behind. Leaders like Nokia, Kodak, etc., who were changing but unfortunately could not disrupt and evolve, went off the radar in a jiffy.

Today even a seventy-year-old is on WhatsApp, though earlier even a forty-year-old would think that he was past the computer age. The words like 'never', 'impossible' and 'unimaginable' are outdated. Brands, which took ages to evolve and establish, are now getting created due to e-commerce and organised retail in just a year and also getting replaced or destroyed equally fast. As new brands are being created daily, everyone is trying hard to stay relevant to the buyer on a sustainable basis. Multinational companies such as Coke and Pepsi are making new brands for different classes of drinks despite being iconic brands.

It was unimaginable even a few years back that a car service provider or hotel service provider could be a global leader without owning a single car or hotel room. And such global leaders have been created in just a few years!

Hence, you should not ever feel that you do not stand a chance against a leader or a giant. Today to defeat someone, you don't need to erase his line or draw a longer line. You just need to create a new colour line which is very distinct from the competitor's line. Putting it simply, you don't need to fight for market share with the competition; you have to just see how to create your own market.

Today's impossibility is tomorrow's reality. Will we do it or someone else will—is our choice. Don't question the fact that things will change; just question the type of change. We need to be on the job of moving ahead and ensure that passiveness and relaxation do not get the better of us. Let the pause not become a full stop.

We should not think that disruption is just in working and business life. It's happening equally fast, if not faster, in our social life. We just need to swing around and see that our children learn to appreciate the pace of things. The way we respond and interact with our most loved ones has undergone a sea of change and is expected to change even more. We talk of industry 4.0 but the reality is that social 4.0 is an equally important concept which needs to be understood to create a society and workforce to handle industry 4.0.

We should also not think that we disrupt by changing things abruptly and quantitatively. We can very well disrupt by evolving on a continuous basis, that is, disruption can also be change x change x change. As we all know that the elevator is not the only way of reaching the top; climbing consistently up the stairs will also take you up there. If we remember the firecrackers of Diwali, there was a garland bomb (called *laree* in Hindi) which was made of many small firecracker sticks and would go unnoticed if burnt separately but when joined together, they created a bigger impact than a chocolate bomb.

Stephen Covey has said, 'To achieve goals you have never achieved before, you need to start doing things you have never done before.'

So then, will you change to disrupt the norm or allow the change to disrupt you?

3

Out-of-Box Thinking

At first, they will ask why you're doing it.
Later they will ask how you did it.
—Anonymous

How do we inculcate the spirit of change and disruption and make it part and parcel of life? I move on to another important mantra of my life which has impacted me in a major way. I have to admit that I learnt this from a class-eight-student. One of my friend's son had written a book in class eight that I read out of obligation for my friend and the boy who wrote a book at this tender age. In one of the chapters, he had described how he presented a school project on Egypt by creating a pyramid and putting all the contents into it. The idea was so simple but still neither had I, nor anyone I knew of, had ever done a project in that fashion. We never went beyond calligraphy, attractive pictures, good cover pages, etc. I asked myself, why hadn't anyone ever thought of doing a school project differently? Why does everyone do it the same way?

I started motivating people to be different and think out of the box. In one of my speeches in an entrepreneurship program, I spoke about the importance of being different and creative. After a month, I got a call from a boy thanking me for motivating him. He shared that he had applied to a famous shoe company for a job and had got a call from the HR head. I instantly congratulated him anticipating he had got the job; however, to my surprise, he said he didn't get the job. I was zapped and confused and asked as to why he had called to thank me. He then said that he was inspired by my speech and thus he had prepared his CV differently by making it in the shape of a shoe sole and putting down his points under various parts of the shoe to show how, like a perfect shoe, he was a perfect candidate for the job. Unfortunately, they had a policy of hiring only those chartered accountants who passed the exam in the first attempt. Hence, he did not get selected. However, the HR head was highly impressed and to ensure that this boy didn't lose this innovative spirit, he called up to praise him for his endeavour.

However, you always won't be appreciated because of your different ways and it may backfire on a few occasions. Hence, always balance your approach and take calculated risks. You may bet 20 per cent and be bold to attempt something different but think twice before betting 80 per cent as very few people can pull it off; but those who do are the ones who are able to create history. Probably that's why most successful people have had many failures behind them and many had nothing to lose which emboldened them to try new, bold and out-of-the-box things.

I will share another story. One of my cousins had to make a presentation in a competition and her idea was related to blind people. I pushed her to do something different and she agreed to give it a try. She blind-folded herself and made a presentation without being able to see the jury and guess the impact she created on the jury.

Many will argue, it is easier said than done. Everyone knows the importance of being different to succeed. Success can never be copied successfully and more so in this VUCA (volatility, uncertainty, complexity and ambiguity) World where changes are on skates and disruption has become a norm. The moot point is how to differentiate successfully; innovation is great, but how?

Firstly, I would like to say that we normally tend to relate innovation to big things in life. However, you can be different in small ways in life. Someone said that great people don't necessarily do different things. Instead, they do things differently.

I would like to share how I changed my style of working and thinking. I ask myself a simple question—'Can I do this differently? Is there another way?' This simple question makes the mind tick and ideas start coming to you. We don't need to be Einstein or Graham Bell to be different. We can find ways in the simple things we do in life. It is just a matter of pausing and giving yourself that extra minute to answer this simple question.

I am going to share a simple thing we agreed as a couple (surprising but sometimes we all do).

My wife is very generous and never misses an opportunity to give some money to a beggar; I always stop her as I strongly feel that due to this generosity, we are creating more beggars for whom it has become a profession. However, I could never answer her as to what is the fault of the ones who have become beggars due to some misfortune. After mulling over it, we found a solution. We bought biscuit packets and kept them in the car. We would open the wrapper and hand over the biscuits so that they would eat them. It worked so well that today so many others have started doing the same and our car became so famous at the crossings that kids would knock at the window and point towards the pockets where biscuits were kept. In life, we can find so many small things to create a difference.

Another big positive impact of it is that it makes you exercise your mind and stops you from becoming a boring, slow and just-following-the-motion-of-life person. There always is an excitement attached around doing something differently and defying the law of 'let's not disturb the norm'.

One needs to build this in the system; everyone isn't born with innovativeness. However, we can always try to build it by trying to think 'out of the box'. We typically resign saying that we don't have it in us, see how talented the other person is and so on. It's a nice way of consoling ourselves and redeeming ourselves from our routine, straight-line thinking. Many people acquit themselves with the saying 'simple thinking, high living'. However, being different doesn't take away your simplicity!

For those who feel down and out because they are not as talented or gifted as others, I am just sharing a small thought:

In the race of life where there are many twists and turns, a Ferrari may lose out to a motorcycle despite having more power and speed as a motorbike can navigate the twists and turns much better.

We all know the hare and the tortoise story so never give up without trying. You just need one good turn and life may take you onto a highway. Whenever you feel like giving up, just pick up and read the story of any great person and you will know there are no success stories without hurdles.

I hope as you read, you are thinking about how to do something differently in your own small way.

You don't need to jump out of the box but surely can wander a bit outside the boundaries and test the waters.

It's very important to understand the difference between commitment and attachment. We typically get so attached to things, thoughts or possessions that we find it difficult to break free and decide objectively. It is important to be committed to whatever you are doing and the cause or objective but do not get attached to the way or system of achieving that. It restricts us from moving beyond the defined boundaries and looking beyond at newer and better options. It is perfectly fine to be committed to our ship but if it starts sinking, we should know when to detach ourselves from the ship and move on before it's too late.

Another important concept, which stifles creativity, is the concept of specialisation versus generalisation. Society has always encouraged and promoted specialisation as it makes it easier to find your niche and acceptability. However, the fast-changing world raises a big question mark on the same. Specialisation is important for the attainment of knowledge; however, it may lead to cognitive bias. Today, being a polymath is probably more relevant as it develops the capability of thinking outside the proverbial box that says it cannot be done. Michael Simmons has defined a modern polymath as 'someone who becomes competent in at least three diverse domains and integrates them into a top one per cent skill set.'

Just remember to ask yourself the question:

'Is there another way of doing it?' Please don't analyse the options before framing them; too much of analysis is a definite paralysis. It is probably why the best entrepreneurs are not the most educated and logical people in the world.

To summarise, the following simple steps can be tried for thinking and acting 'out of the box':

- Mindset change—accept the importance of change and agree that doing things differently is important to succeed and shine.
- Ask yourself every day, how I can do my work and activities differently?
- Don't fear to do things differently.

- Remember, failures are the pillars of success; so don't give up if you fail or even lose in the process of differentiation.
- Keep looking around you and see what has made others succeed; it will keep motivating you.
- Success encourages but failures teach. Keep trying with calculated risks to bring changes and disruptions around us so that people follow us.
- Break free from the shackles of preconceived notions as they inhibit our action and thoughts.

I would like to end this chapter with what Jeff Bezos, Amazon, said: 'I am frequently asked the question of what's going to change in the next 10 years, but almost never asked what's not going to change in next 10 years.' The truth is that almost everything will change, so the box within which you are comfortable will move ahead, leaving you behind, if you don't start using your creative visualisation powers to stay a step ahead.

4

Be a Professional

Being a professional is doing the things you love to do, on the days you don't feel like doing them.

—Julius Erving

We normally attribute this word to our working lives in the office. We discuss and deliberate on how to be more professional in our work approach and there is a premium tag attached to those who qualify to be called professionals. We compare cities and their style of working and tag them as professional or unprofessional.

Unfortunately, very few understand the real meaning of the word 'professional'. Professional is nothing more than a person who works with a certain attitude, mindset and system. You don't have to be educated to be a professional; you just need to work systematically, logically and follow basic processes. Anything that makes a task easier, faster and closer to perfection is a step towards being professional.

Even a student can study professionally if the student plans, strategises and studies systematically rather than being ad hoc while learning and understanding things. Two students with almost similar IQ and hours of studies will see different results and output because of the way they spent those studying hours.

Let's simplify it further. Mr A goes to and fro, from point X to Y, five times, because he doesn't plan and complete his work at one point before moving to the next point. He keeps going up and down, which, apart from the loss of time, leads to loss of energy. On the other hand, Mr B completes all pending work at Point X and then moves to Point Y. Here, Mr B is more professional than Mr A, though both are good at their work and equally capable.

Another example is of two ladies, both responsible for maintaining their homes. One couples it up with part-time working while the other spends a good part of the day doing only house chores. Both are great housewives and mothers but there is a difference in the way they work. That difference is what we may call professionalism, that is, one does housework and manages a career while the other spends full time on housework.

The moot point, which I want to highlight, is that always try to plan work better by being more professional in your approach. The question is, how can one do so much in twenty-four hours?

Discipline, planning, strategising and a positive mindset are some of the hallmarks of professionalism and are some of the key attributes of being successful in life.

Professionalism, like other positive attributes, has to be built in our DNA. It has to be an approach and style of our life rather than something ad hoc, which we keep planning and implementing. It is related to work but in the true sense of the word, it is something that is important in every activity and encompasses our entire daily routine.

Along with hard work, which is important, smart work cannot be undermined. Humans are different from other living beings due to their mental prowess. To be differentiated among themselves, they need to use the same properly.

Therefore, besides thinking if there is any other way of doing things, let us also start asking if there is a 'better' way of doing something. We can consider effective multitasking as a sign of professionalism as it leads to time-bound and effective execution of work.

They say time is limited and cannot be expanded. It is true, we cannot change the seconds and minutes but we can expand the utility and capacity of each unit of time. The capacity and power of every moment of our life can be enhanced by professionally managing the same.

The quantity of time we have is limited and the same for all. However, we can improve the quality of the time we have. I personally travel a lot for which I cannot spend the same time which most of my friends spend with their family. It was a predicament for me and the thought always bothered me, especially when we read about the need to balance family and work. I finally found my solution to this dilemma by deciding to improve the quality of time I spend with my family. I try to spend Saturday evenings and Sundays as well as public holidays with my family, even if it means travelling back and forth. Further, I ensure that we enjoy every minute by socialising, interacting, talking and entertaining ourselves. I feel it's better than being together yet being separated by TV, technology and worries. I bury my worries, anxiety and tension on Saturday evenings and engage myself in a different world of fun and excitement that extends till Monday morning. It sounds difficult but my friends and family can vouch how quality can compensate for quantity.

In the office, smart work is as important as hard work. Similarly, at home, the quality of engagement is as important as the quantity of time spent. Just doing something for long hours is no proof of success and results.

My WhatsApp status says, '*I am not busy. I just have work.*' Busyness is just a state of mind which reduces our effectiveness and leads to just stress and tension. We need to be calm and functional to ensure that we effectively fulfil our responsibilities across the various spheres of life.

Professionalism = Hard Work + Smart Work

Let's be professional in every walk of life.

5

Multitasking

The secret to multitasking is that it isn't actually multitasking. It's just extreme focus and organization.
—Joss Whedon

Life is getting more complicated with the advent of technology. At any point in time, our contact with the environment has grown multifold due to technology. We have many contact points simultaneously through phone, email, Facebook, Twitter, WhatsApp and so on. Earlier, our work hours used to end as soon as we left the office. However, now almost every job has become a twenty-four-hour service. We may be contacted anytime for any work.

The pressures and demands have grown, with every contact point expecting prompt response and action. Everyone forgets that the mind is still single, which despite its immense power, has problems in jumping from one issue to another in split seconds. The time in which we would earlier have made one communication, today probably we are doing ten of them. The rebounds and replies are equally fast, multiplying the demands on us.

We find only once in a while people taking a social media vacation, switching off their mobiles or cutting themselves off from the internet. However, most of us cannot do the same and it may not even be desirable. This is taking a toll on us, leading to fading memories, mental tiredness, high blood pressure and other ailments cropping up due to stress and tension.

The question is, how do we satisfactorily handle the new demands of work and life? How do we effectively cope with the multiple demands on us in the same time period? How do we find time for ourselves?

The answer, as you might have guessed from the title of the chapter, is learning to multitask. In fact, more than learning, it is training ourselves to do the same. We need to devise ways we find comfortable to sort out the multiple tasks that are thrown at us from all around. Blocking the access points to us may be a short-term solution but in today's world of speed, we have no choice if we want to stay in the game.

At times it is better to do 80 to 90 per cent of many tasks rather than 100 per cent of one and ignore the rest. We may not be called perfectionists but we may be more successful and up-to-date on the aggregate. 1 x 3 = 3 but it's still less than 0.80 x 5 = 4.

I am regularly asked how I handle so many things so effectively (or at least they feel I am doing so). I would like to share some things which I have started practising to keep up with the pace of this world.

I have introduced Skype or video conferencing in many associations where I am involved, so that I can cut travel time. Simultaneously, by muting, I am able to take short calls in between such meetings without being impolite and also reply to short emails or messages.

Even when we need to travel, we can utilise time effectively by working as if in office by replying to emails, messages and calls. You don't have to be in the office to do work. You can clear most of your desk even when on the move. Documents on the table can be emailed, WhatsApped and suitably answered. At least 90 per cent of emails don't need more than a few quick lines of reply so I flag the ones needing time and clear the balance. Even when I am out of the office for a week, I can clear my table in less than an hour.

We can afford to be more informal in our regular communication (except some of the very important ones where we need to be very formal) to save time and energy. In the time one formal reply is made like a letter, we can reply to multiple emails. Salutations and long sentences can be avoided where we are dealing with friends, employees and regularly connected people. It's a matter of choice but I prefer to complete ten emails rather than one formal email.

Even this book was difficult to write with so many things happening around me, so I decided to write the same on flights where I was cut off from the external world.

We need to move from the quantity of time spent working and move to the quality of time we spend. Work will always expand to the time we have so when we work, we need to be professional, effective and quick. As said earlier, with hard work, we need to do smart work to be successful in life.

It is also a matter of better planning so we bunch up similar tasks that can be completed at one go more effectively rather than doing them in bits and pieces.

The thought which will arise in your mind is, everyone doesn't have a sharp enough mind to do multiple things at one go; they need focus to do things well. I agree, but most things we do during our day don't need equal levels of focus and can be combined. A lady while cooking can serially do her work or while the dish is being cooked, she can simultaneously complete other side chores. It is more a matter of attitude and awareness to multitask so that you get more time out of the kitchen.

Also, to be a good multitasker, you need a fresh, calm, and alert mind. This can only come if we sleep well, take power naps and breathe deeply when agitated. If you can get yourself to meditate regularly, there is nothing to beat that.

Even a simple thing like exercising can be combined with fresh air and sun by doing the same in a garden or balcony rather than in an air-conditioned gym.

Please don't write it off as something not possible for you. Try at least for a day to multitask and see whether you increase your potential to do more things in a shorter span of time. There are many things which can be done parallelly instead of sequentially. We just need to be aware and alert for the same. Whoever you are, time in a day will never exceed twenty-four hours. However, our mode of utilising the same will differentiate us. We must have seen that the same amount of work is done in different time spans by different people; partly it is better efficiency and partly it is due to multitasking. Trust me, it's easier to multitask than improve actual efficiency; so we can still beat other people through better planning and execution.

Let's make our twenty-four hours into forty-eight hours instead of twelve hours; it will give us four times more life to live. We shall have so much more time to make our life a beautiful rainbow with great colours.

Multitasking is one of the most important elements of professionalism and multiplies one of the most limited resources of our life, that is, time.

Time = Output achieved, not the number of hours.

The orange is the same but how much juice we shall squeeze from it without spoiling the taste depends on an individual.

It's interesting that recently I spotted a calendar that had a mention of the lifestyles of three eminent and successful people. I am sharing the same with you below:

Elon Musk (Tesla): 'His mantra is to do the most of the things at once. He emails while scanning documents, holds video calls while having lunch, and texts while his children are on his lap.'

Bill Gates (Microsoft): 'Do more in less time. Work on a multi-monitor display to manage emails like him. He uses one screen for inbox, one for current emails, and one for regular work.'

Sundar Pichai (Google): 'Wakes up early and does multitasking—while brushing his teeth, he checks his emails. Works in quiet and large spaces, which boosts his productivity.'

Multitasking is a contentious activity and is not recommended by many as they feel that it leads to a lack of focus and a lot of chaos in life that leads to substandard results. I fully agree that we need to be judicious in deciding the extent and degree of multitasking. There are many important activities which need 100 per cent focus and attention and should not be mixed with other jobs. However, there are, for sure, many simple things which can be coordinated and done parallelly.

I Hope tomorrow you will surely take one step forward to multitasking and create that extra time and space in your life to fulfil your dreams. The suitcase is the same for all of us, how much we can stuff in it depends on the individual.

6

Need to Ask the Right Questions

The man who asks a question is a fool for a minute, the man who does not ask is a fool for life.

—Phil M Jones

We always tend to feel that knowing the answers is the most important thing in life. However, I feel, to reach there, it is very important to ask the right questions. Our education system prebuilds the notion in us that the questions are given and we just need to know the answers. However, as we get out of this standard old system of education and step out into the real world, we understand the importance of asking questions.

Once I got over the standard school and college life and stepped into IIM Ahmedabad to do my MBA, I realised that learning involved asking the 'right questions' as answers were not always available in the textbooks. I realised that there is so much knowledge and information around us that to draw from the same, we need to understand and question. The answers came flowing from professors, peers, learning groups, etc. This has become more relevant today with the availability of the internet and the whole new digital world.

In Google, if we type our questions properly, we get the answers. They are mostly there but we need to ask the questions properly and accurately. Today, we are living in a world of information and knowledge. The answers are all around us but to seek and find them, we need to know precisely what we want to know or else it is just a flow of tons of information which confuses rather than clarifying our concepts. Some institutions have started open-book examinations. Even though they give you a book full of answers, very few are able to find it.

Now a simple question may come to your mind as to how do we ask the right questions? It surely isn't as simple as it sounds. My first simple advice is 'don't be afraid to ask questions'. Most of the time the fear of being ridiculed and laughed at stops us from asking the right questions. I am sure if you go back to your school and college days, you will recall moments when you wanted to know something but didn't ask out of fear of what your peers may say, for instance, 'You don't even know this!'

We prefer to stay ignorant for life rather than face a few people who themselves may not know the answers. We need to get rid of the syndrome of what others will think of us and develop confidence in ourselves. If you don't believe in yourself, how can you expect others to believe in you?

Life isn't a platform or racetrack where we need to be winners all the time. It is more of a place to experience, learn and live. Winning or losing is just a subset of the same and we will have those ups and downs throughout our lives.

If you are still not convinced, look around and see the people who normally move ahead in life—the bold ones who fear not to fail or the ones who are always just trying to seem good, right and intelligent? Is seeming to be knowledgeable more important than being one?

Please don't think I am pushing you to be a child who is inquisitive by nature and keeps asking small things. If you start behaving like that, you won't find people around you to answer (Google, of course, would still be there). However, don't bury your knowledge and understanding filling gaps by artificial layers of intelligence and arrogance. Not all questions will be appropriate and correct but who is always right? The more you ask, the more you understand and the more chances you have of getting close to the answers.

Be polite and patient in your asking. Don't be pushy, but DO ASK.

In IIM, many subjects had marks for class participation. As I had come from a one-way system of learning, I found this irritating and unfair as all participants didn't have equal communication skills. However, I later realised, the essence wasn't just to know how much you knew but to get you out of the shell and push you to discuss and question concepts and situations. The group discussions also helped as I was a bit more comfortable in a small group of friends.

I have gone through this whole process myself—of not asking due to shyness and fear and then slowly realising that it is better to take the risk of being ridiculed or found weird once rather than being ignorant for life. Not knowing would probably cost me more in life when I really need the answer.

Another important perspective of asking questions is that it leads to explaining things to people using reverse psychology. Many a times, better than trying to convince people, it's better to ask them the questions that make them think about the answers and in the process understand things better. This also breaks the wall of ego and supremacy, as rather than being dictated, you're being queried and in the process being acknowledged to be superior. This can be used very effectively by parents, bosses and teachers at a small cost of acknowledging 'I do not know. Can you explain?' For example, if a parent tells their child that a particular course is not appropriate for him or her, it is met with resistance. However, if a parent asks the child why he or she is choosing this course and what are the pros and cons, this will lead to a healthy discussion initiated by the child. There is a good chance that the views of both will converge. The question, if framed properly will lead to a structured and healthy analysis.

Keep asking to keep learning and understanding.

7

Always Be a Student

You begin learning in the womb and go right on learning until the moment you pass on. Your brain has a capacity for learning that is virtually limitless, which makes every human a potential genius.

—Michael J. Gelb

When we complete our education, there is a great sense of relief. It is the day we have waited for years as we have got tired of the endless routine of examinations. We wait for that day when we feel that we have learnt enough and it's time to go out and use our learning and knowledge to be successful in life and earn a living for ourselves.

However, we are all in for a nasty surprise. The process of learning never seems to end. We suddenly feel that most of what we have learnt isn't relevant in the real world and we once again have to learn or re-learn to make ourselves relevant and capable of performing real-life tasks. We are guided partly by our seniors and mentors. Yet there are many things that we have to learn by looking around and observing how others are performing. The examinations are no more time-bound and announced but rear their heads every now and then.

It is at this point we understand that learning never stops. We never stop being a student though the label has gone by years ago. There may not be any so-called teachers and books but everything around us is teaching us on an ongoing basis. This has become more relevant today where the world is on a fast track and the environment is changing faster than what we can imagine.

As discussed in the earlier chapters, change is permanent and slowly, disruption is becoming a norm. The concept of thinking and doing 'out of the box' is becoming more and more relevant. In such a situation where we need to keep doing new things in new ways, we have to keep learning and doing self-teaching. We don't realise but like the moving earth, things are changing every moment. However, we only realise when the night sets in, that is, when things have darkened for us because we didn't accept and notice the change. Learning ensures that we be a polymath, a person with diverse domain skills that help us engage better in this fast-changing world.

Again, I must confess that it is easier said than done. However, do we have a choice? Honestly speaking, we don't, so let's move on and try. How can one make it a habit to keep learning? Well, there are many ways of doing the same, like reading progressive books, keeping good and knowledgeable company, spending time listening and learning about things that are not directly relevant to us and attending workshops/seminars/short courses in established institutions. We need to take out some time from our daily routine and invest it for the future; ensure that the mind is ticking and thinking and not placid.

Just as we take out time for our health, hobbies and enjoyment, we must also allocate time for our mind. A strong, energised and positive mindset is important for every aspect of our life. Most of us go to the gym for staying in good health or diet but very few look for a gym for our mind. We don't realise that if the mind isn't healthy, our body can never be. We have seen cases of how depression impacts our physical health more than a physical ailment does.

Give time to your mind, brain and thinking faculties. Let them grow to stay ahead of times and create faculties and a knowledge base to lead the world boldly and confidently.

Don't always look for a one-to-one benefit for attending a great lecture or courses in top institutes, etc. Just as you can't see the impact of every healthy food you eat, similarly don't expect every iota of knowledge and learning to manifest visibly in your daily life. We need a balanced diet of vitamins, carbohydrates, proteins and fat and similarly, we need knowledge, learning, insights and motivation in a balanced proportion to develop the faculties, which will create the right platform and ground for the seeds to be sown for a fantastic and great life.

A student who wants to be a businessman may find physics and chemistry irrelevant. However, the basic knowledge ingrained in those early days helps us appreciate and understand when our managers try to explain technical things related to our products. Similarly, biology may have nothing to do with business but when we discuss our health, the basic knowledge of the human body becomes relevant. Basic knowledge gained in our education over the twelve to fourteen years of schooling helps us in overall development though 90 per cent of the things learnt cannot be matched with what we do in life. Yet if you compare an uneducated person with an educated person, you can see the visible difference. In short, one would say that no learning or experience is wasted. If you look carefully, you shall surely find a way to make them all add up.

Learning is also an art and we need to know what and when to learn. I am sure most of us never understood the significance of history but we can learn immensely by reading about the lives of great people if we understand and learn from their perspectives. Unfortunately, 90 per cent of the questions revolve around insignificant things like dates and names and very rarely do we talk about the learnings, experiences and the style of working and living. The most important lesson has been restricted to a by-product of the way we have conceptualised our subject learning.

Most people feel we missed opportunities to learn in life and now it is too late. Today with multiple options all around us, it is never too late. We may not have cracked CAT and got admission into a decent MBA institute, but who can stop us from going and attending an executive programme in any of the IIMs? The same professors and the same course content are there for us. If we still feel that we are too busy to take out time for even a week's residential course, we have so many options to learn online.

Today, learning is limited just by our desire; hence, one should keep the learning wheel moving. Learning is an ongoing process; like a magnet, we need to keep pulling knowledge and information towards us.

Just read another pertinent quote on the Facebook wall of my friend and author Dr Shalini Lal: 'Staying relevant will become almost a fulltime job. You will need to keep learning and reinventing yourself. The day you stop is the day you need to be very worried.'

It may sound weird, but there is learning even in giving knowledge and sharing experience. I am a regular mentor to various business start-ups and youth and I have always learnt something new while interacting to share my knowledge. It is so true that giving is also gaining. My new social venture, BiznessClinic is motivated by the urge to share my learnings and experience with businessmen by mentoring them there, but in the process, I shall be enriched with the wisdom and experience of my mentees.

So friends, let us keep an open and receptive mind. Let us never ever get into the mode of 'we know everything' or 'we missed the learning opportunities'. You may have known everything till yesterday (though that's also doubtful), but unless you allow new things to flow in, you will be ignorant of the changes of today and tomorrow. Even when you make a house, you need to keep repairing it, as cracks and gaps are inevitable even in the best of houses.

8

Problems Are Learning Opportunities

A pessimist sees the difficulty in every opportunity; an optimist sees the opportunity in every difficulty.

—Winston Churchill

We all fear problems and the very inkling of the same puts us down. Problems are no doubt a source of worry but just like other things in life, it is something we cannot avoid. Big and small problems just keep surfacing as we drive down the road of life. Even the best of roads will have small potholes and if nothing, there will be road bumps built to check our pace and slow us down.

However, it is true that our mind and heart decide how big a problem is. It can magnify a problem and make a hill out of a mole and vice versa. Hence, internal strength and courage are very important to face and resolve a problem. There may be a business problem which will need to be confronted on Monday morning and there is nothing we can do about it on the weekend. However, we spoil our weekend by allowing it to expand into our thoughts and surface, again and again, knowing very well that there is nothing we can do about it before Monday.

Problems will always take us back and impair us in some fashion. However, it is important that we don't allow it to get the better of us. We can't ignore them as they have to be tackled and resolved; sweeping them under the carpet just allows them to get bigger.

A school friend who topped IIT Entrance Exams, recently shared on Facebook: 'It's amazing to find out that in a different guise, nearly every problem that one encounters has already been solved by someone else, though the solution may exist in a different form and domain.' I agree that there is a solution to a problem, it's just that we need to learn and seek the same.

Hence, I would like to share another dimension of a problem which has helped me considerably in handling the same. I must give the credit for this to an IIMA professor who managed to sow this deep into me.

Problems, apart from being a headache, are also a learning experience and opportunity. Every problem we go through makes us more capable as we learn how to tackle the same. I remember in the early days of my career, I faced a problem and was sweating. I cannot discuss the problem and solution here but it was something that would let my company down in an international exhibition in Dubai. I just told myself to focus on the solution and for sure there has to be one. The thought that once I resolve it, I would have learnt something and be a better person, gave me the courage and push and with a few hiccups, I did find the solution and saved the day.

Another example that I would like to share is of two businesses: one had a dream run and the other was unfortunate to face various tax and regulatory issues. They both grew and after ten years, they both faced a big legal problem. The one who had no experience of handling complicated legal problems was badly hit by it and almost closed down. The other person was used to it and took it in his stride and kept moving on. The luck of having a dream run proved counterproductive as he missed the learnings that a problem teaches and was unable to cope when a big one came. The confidence of a man who has faced and solved problems is backed by conviction and experience while that of a man who has had a smooth run in life is somewhere hollow inside.

It is funny but true that even problems are important in life and part and parcel of living and growing. This is probably the reason why greatest and successful people have had their extraordinary share of problems and failures.

Those who feel disheartened when results are not positive just remember the story of the ant that kept climbing and falling but finally did scale the wall. And if still you feel low, just pick up and read the story of your personal hero or iconic figure. You will understand and believe the saying, 'Failures are the pillars of success'.

One last thought, problems are problems till we don't have a solution. Heat or cold isn't an issue if we have an air conditioner or heater; so learn from the problem, seek a solution and erase the problem forever from your life.

Hence, let's also toast to our problems because they will lead us to our real successes. They are a real teacher and ensure we always remain a student, learning about the infinite situations that life can present us.

I would like to end with a small story about how problems can become our strength and source of motivation.

The Japanese have a great liking for fresh fish. But the waters close to Japan have not held many fishes for decades. So, to feed the Japanese population, fishing boats got bigger and went farther than ever.

The farther the fishermen went, the longer it took to bring back the fishes. The longer it took them to bring back the fishes, the staler they grew. So, fishing companies installed fish tanks. They would catch the fishes and stuff them in the tanks, fin to fin. After a little hashing around, fishes stopped moving. They were tired and dull, but alive. Unfortunately, the Japanese could still taste the difference. Because the fishes did not move for days, they lost their fresh-fish taste. The Japanese preferred the lively taste of fresh fish, not the sluggish fish. The fishing industry faced an impending crisis!

To keep the fishes tasting fresh, the Japanese fishing companies continue to put the fishes in tanks. But now they add a small shark to each tank. The shark eats a few fishes, but most of the fishes arrive in a very lively state. The fishes are challenged and hence are constantly on the move. And they survive and arrive in a healthy state. The challenge they face, keeps them fresh!

Humans are no different. L. Ron Hubbard observed in the early 1950s: 'Man thrives, oddly enough, only in the presence of a challenging environment.' George Bernard Shaw said: 'Satisfaction is death!'

If you are steadily conquering challenges, you are happy. Your challenges keep you energised. They keep you alive!

Put a shark in your tank and see how far you can really go—problems are not only an opportunity to learn but also a constant push to us to move ahead in life.

9

Hope Is No Strategy

You pile up enough tomorrows, and you'll find you are left with nothing but a lot of empty yesterdays.
—Harold Hill

It surprises me, but when I look around and talk to business people, I find that hope is a very important business strategy for most. Often, when times are bad and the chips are down, they keep hoping that the law of averages will set in and things will improve on their own. I can't really blame them as in the past they have seen things changing suddenly for the better and profits going up. Hence, they feel that just tightening the seat belts and waiting for good times is a good option.

They keep hoping that tomorrow will be better and shining. There isn't any logic or rationale to the same but they keep hoping and hoping. I wouldn't say hope is a bad thing because it keeps one motivated and upbeat in bad times. However, we should not forget that karma is very important in life and we must keep trying and pushing ourselves towards a better tomorrow. We should never give up and as discussed earlier, we need to change with times and think differently to race ahead of the competition. The saying 'God helps those who help themselves' should always be kept in mind. Destiny and God are there to help us but unless we push the accelerator, how will the car race ahead? We have automatic cars nowadays so gear changing isn't necessary, but still, we need to control the brake and accelerator.

It is advocated in many philosophies and thoughts that karma is the architect of our destiny. Hence, hope without karma isn't complete. Hope needs to push us to make that extra effort rather than being the cause of leaving everything to destiny. There is rarely a one-to-one relationship between effort and fruits but cumulatively at some point in time, we shall get what we sow. We cannot put it into an algebra equation but life is a great leveller and I am sure most of us have experienced it.

Anyway, it is way beyond the scope of this book to discuss the theory of karma and destiny. However, I just want to drive home the point that one should not sit back and wait for things to improve; don't just hope. Understand, analyse and decide the course of action to fight any downtrend. We cannot control the external environment but we can surely change our internal environment. Maybe we can't get better prices for our products but we can surely reduce our costs.

There is one thing I can vouch for. There is always the scope of improvement in whatever we are doing. Even if we are the best today, tomorrow the changing environment may make us the second best unless we stay aware and awake and keep evaluating, reviewing and readjusting ourselves. It sounds difficult but if the same becomes part of our systems, processes and DNA, then it will happen effortlessly.

Change is as much a routine as other daily chores.

Hope may fail us but positive karma will never fail us. Everyone can't climb Mount Everest but everyone can definitely be better than what they were yesterday.

Let's not wait in the forest for the rain to come; let's just dig the ground till we find water. Everything we need is always around us; it is just that we need to find it rather than hoping for it to find us. The faith and hope that it is there should drive us to search and locate it. Hence, hope can be a positive factor if it motivates us to do deeds but dangerous when it puts us in a passive and pause mode.

I would like to share a small story before concluding. There were two traders Mr A and Mr B. They traded in the stock markets regularly. Mr A and Mr B both bought shares of X Company as they thought it would rise. They bought 1,000 shares at ₹1,000 in the Futures market, expecting it would go to ₹2,000 based on a strong tip they received from a friend. However, due to some negative news, the prices started falling. Mr B sold off at ₹900 and booked a loss of ₹1 lakh as soon as he heard the news. Mr A held on as he was hopeful that the news was wrong and the price would correct soon. The price fell to ₹600 and Mr A did not have the courage to cut losses as he would incur a huge loss. He kept waiting and hoping every day that the price would turn around at some point and maybe like Mr B, he would be able to reduce his loss. However, it kept falling and reached ₹300 and incurred a heavy loss of ₹7 lakh. He did not have the capacity to afford more losses and had to finally square up his position at ₹300.

This is a common story with which many would relate to. We keep hoping while defying logic and common sense and finally, things reach a stage of breakdown. If we do not create and control our environment, it will start controlling and creating you.

I would like to end with a small story I heard at a conference. The speaker's son had fever while others in the family were perfectly fit. He said, the doctor said it was due to the weather but he disagreed as—if weather was the reason then everyone in the family should have fallen ill, if not neighbours too. He said, the real reason was the poor immunity of his son against that of others around him. He further said, similarly in life we face problems in the same environment, while others do not because we have not made ourselves internally strong enough to face and fight the conditions around us. The moral is, do not keep blaming external conditions, which are not in our control, hoping we shall be safe. Instead, work on developing your inner resilience and strength that will hold you in good stead at all times in life.

10

Karma or Destiny

Never stop fighting until you arrive at your destined place—that is, the unique you. Have an aim in life, continuously acquire knowledge, work hard and have perseverance to realise the great life.

—APJ Abdul Kalam

This is probably the most discussed topic in life and we leave many things to or place blame for them on destiny. There are numerous times we leave things to fate or resign to destiny when we don't succeed. It is difficult to say whether it is done to justify the failures or really one strongly believes in the same. Most balanced people give weightage to both karma/deeds/actions and destiny.

We all understand karma but what exactly is destiny or fate? It is said that it's pre-written in life.

Some call it the will of God while others say it is both God's will and the result of the deeds of our past lives.

One beautiful explanation given by someone is: 'God doesn't decide your fate or destiny; it is your own karma which you aggregate and the same is returned to you at an appropriate time. God is a supreme power but can someone who we worship and respect wish or do bad to anyone? God is just like a bank manager who keeps account of your good and bad deeds and returns your deposits to you. Sometimes, he may provide overdraft facilities but ultimately, everything has to be balanced.'

Anyway, my idea isn't to get into this discussion and try to find the universal truth of God, destiny and karma. It is beyond the scope of my prowess or ability and probably there is no universal truth known to mankind. There are just perspectives shared by various enlightened souls who have blessed this world at different points of time. The reason for discussion is just to share a perspective of how we could balance all these thoughts to move forward and succeed in life.

It is very clear that if our future is pre-written, there isn't much we can do about it as it is surely not written by a pencil that can be erased by us. Most believe that it's God's will and so only God can change it. Hence, we do various pujas, etc. to request him to change things in our favour. I have nothing against it and being a believer of God myself, I see no harm in remembering and worshipping a supreme being. However, here again, we don't know whether our prayers will be heard or God will design as per our wishes/ request.

The basic thing is that the same isn't in our control, hence let's focus on things that we can alter and which will probably help us in moving ahead. Further, we can't deny the fact that every guru or motivator or acharya always motivates us to do good deeds, which means that there is definitely an important role of the same in our lives. The debate/ discussion on whether it helps our immediate life or goes into building our destiny will carry on but surely it has a very important role in our lives.

Similarly, our karmas do play an important role in shaping and structuring our life. It may not be always visible or directly matched with the outcomes but it is still there. We can never see or identify salt in a dish but it is still a very important input to it and the dish would be incomplete without that '*pinch of salt*'.

I firmly believe that life and its cycle is a science that is beyond human beings to fully comprehend but we should have faith in its logic and systems and give it our best. Let's stop worrying about things we can't change or control, let's focus on things we can surely change. Let's make a difference and leave our mark.

The accelerator in a car is given but the speed of the car depends on how hard we press the accelerator. Hence, even if Lady Luck is shining on us, we need to make the most while the sun is shining. Everyone gets equal sun but some harness solar energy and get the most out of it while some even struggle for Vitamin D.

This can be linked to the earlier chapter on 'hope is no strategy', hence, let's focus on things we can do. Positive thinking and attitude are very important and as we cannot see beyond a bend or curve, let us not assume that only bad times or good times will continue. Our vision is limited, so let us try to do things that are in our control and not assume or presume things and give up.

I would like to share a simple example which most of us will be able to relate to. The deck of cards which are distributed in a game can be attributed as destiny. However, how we use and play them is our karma. Fate can put us in a situation but still, we have the choice of deciding how to handle it.

Lastly, just rewind and remember all the good and bad surprises we have got in life, especially the times we got more than our expectations and this will remind you that trying can take you anywhere. Personally, I never thought I would top the best MBA school of India and be able to take on the bright IIT students; in fact, I joined IIMA with just enough conviction that I would pass. However, I was pleasantly shocked to see myself as a forerunner and eventually passing out as a gold medallist. Life has taught me that anything and everything is possible if we keep pushing and working in the right direction. Our capabilities may be limited for 'one/something' but can never be limited for being successful in life.

We must play our roles in full earnestness and with sincerity. Success may be delayed but can never be denied. Talent is given (most cannot recognise the same), but hard work is yours. Life is a combo and needs a blend of everything to succeed and lead.

Karma improves the probability of attaining our goals and objectives of life. The concept of constantly improving our probability to succeed is an important perspective.

We have heard of so many success stories of school dropouts like Bill Gates, which we tend to quote so many times to prove that just getting good marks does not make you successful. We most probably would not be personally knowing Bill Gates but for sure would have seen and known many below-par performers making it really big in life.

Does it mean we can conclude that it's not important to perform well in school and strive for better marks, ranks and degrees? Most study as a means or route to be successful in life. If it had no correlation, then probably many would have given up studying much earlier in life.

Similarly, there are many smokers who live till the age of ninety while many disciplined, health-conscious people die due to cancer at sixty years of age. There are many who can drink till eighty while teetotallers are dying of heart attacks at fifty.

Many use such exceptional examples to justify their actions and have a feel-good factor. The truth is that nothing we do can guarantee us anything in life. We live in a world of probabilities and in every minute our actions endeavour to improve our chances of success, that is, the probability that we shall achieve our goals is higher. The number of CEOs of top companies in the USA who are from Ivy League colleges is high, but it does not mean that ordinary college students cannot be CEOs.

Every positive action of ours improves our probability to succeed and achieve. There is a story that says that a monkey who chose a stock portfolio by throwing darts at stock choices performed a bit better than a portfolio created by investment experts. However, it does not mean that we should do away with experts and randomly choose our portfolio. It's true that our portfolio may perform better but the probability of the same happening is much less than a portfolio prepared by an investment expert.

Hence, let's not get swayed by such one-off stories and stop working positively towards our objectives and goals of life. Let's not allow failures and disappointments to belittle the hard and good work done by us to attain and fulfil our dreams. Every positive effort of ours makes us more capable and efficient, which will ultimately take us closer to our destination.

I hope we all give the above thoughts a moment and ask ourselves: 'What can we do today, rather than rue over what we don't have today?' Be assured our actions of today will surely increase the odds of reaching our desired destiny sooner than later.

Even Lord Krishna has said in Bhagwad Gita that keep doing your karma/deeds without worrying about the fruits, your karma will be rewarded by God at the opportune time.

11

Share Things That Don't Cost

If we have no peace, it is because we have forgotten that we belong to each other.

—Mother Teresa

Resources are always limited and in this finite world, we can never have infinite resources. There is always a bottom to every well. Hence, it is natural that we can't always share everything we have with people. Sharing is good but unfortunately, it has to be measured and the flow needs to be controlled by a tap. We are motivated to give but the question sought by a common man is how much can we? We need to first take care of our needs. It may sound selfish but that's the truth.

However, the good news is that there are things which we can share endlessly without worrying that we don't have enough. It sounds odd in this finite world but luckily, we are all blessed by many infinite powers and resources.

Many think that giving and receiving is a zero-sum game but give it a thought and you will see giving as a multiplier. We are so bogged down by the monetary angle that we always relate to 'giving' with money. It is great if we can part with materialistic things but let's not feel dejected if we don't have enough or for some reason are not able to share the same. Life has given us so much more.

So, what are they? It is a very simple but powerful concept.

Smiles, blessings, greetings, appreciation, feedback, sorry, thank you and knowledge are just a few things in the long list which we can share and give without worrying. They are simple and yet so powerful for the receiver.

I know it sounds very obvious and we all know it. But how many practise it? And how long and how much can we do by practising knowingly and won't it become a burden on our free flow behaviour? Yes, it will and hence again, it has to be built into our personality and inner core.

Spreading positivity is the best thing we can do and that's what great and learned personalities keep doing. They share thoughts, ideas and knowledge to motivate and inspire us positively. They are, with every moment, being enriched spiritually and they grow every time they share with us.

Let's just share a few ideas of giving which we all can practise. While travelling, we come across people who are struggling with their bags, who need a seat in the bus to the aeroplane, need a trolley or require assistance to find their way. We can help them with very little effort and it gives a very deep sense of satisfaction. Since I have realised this, I am always happy to get a chance to help in small ways, losing nothing but still giving!

Feedback is normally perceived as criticism, which we consider as constructive without realising the impact on others. We forget there is something as positive feedback which may be a word of appreciation, a pat on the back or just a thumbs up. We do it the whole day on WhatsApp but how many times do we do it in normal life? Just think about the power of reinforcement when someone appreciates you and tells you that you are good.

Most of us have forgotten the power of a smile; it can change so many things and brighten up the life of someone. A simple sorry can change the equations of many relationships. Do we lose anything by answering the questions we know? A smile with a greeting or a thank you doubles the impact.

When a stranger wishes us in the elevator, we are impressed but we rarely initiate it. When a friend's child cheerfully says hello, we tell our children to do the same but we never tell ourselves to do it. We see things with open eyes, agree fully but still never think about them in our context.

I don't want you to just agree with my thoughts, but at least for a week, try to live it in whatever best way each one of you deems fit. Let's try to break the walls of ego, pride, superiority and superficiality which we unknowingly build around us. This stops the free flow of our beautiful inner core which can spread eternal light all across.

I must submit honestly that despite all the awareness, I am far from building the DNA of giving in me. However, I am trying and will keep trying to let the inner core flow out positively and spread across.

Someone will say, what's the big deal in sharing when it doesn't cost us anything? Well, if it is not a big deal, please do it regularly. It doesn't mean that we don't give things which pinch or cost us; I am just saying at least give where it doesn't cost.

We are endowed with a mind that has knowledge and experience. Let's use it fruitfully to help others grow. We can be instrumental without actually donating money for others to gain much more, if we can mentor and motivate them to multiply their resources.

I was recently there with a friend on the death of his father. I suggested him to donate his father's eyes which he agreed to and that led two people to gain vision within just twenty-four hours. A simple suggestion led to a good deed. Our constant motivation and the flow of positive ideas can lead to many such good deeds—a clear win-win situation.

I have personally experienced so much positivity which flows inside me when I mentor and guide the youth. It has never been a one-way traffic road.

I have always learnt and experienced new facts from mentees. It's a really enriching experience, yet people don't want to even share that with people who need it. As discussed earlier, we are always a student, the learning never stops and many call it 'givers' gain'.

I will like to share a small story of how giving means receiving.

A speaker at a workshop gave each attendee one balloon, asking them to write their name on it with a marker pen and place it in a small adjacent room. Once all were done, he said, 'I give you five minutes. Quickly go into the room and find the balloon with your name on it. The ones who do it first will win.'

Everyone was frantically searching for their balloon, colliding with each other, pushing others around and there was utter chaos. At the end of those five minutes, only ten people found their balloons.

The speaker said, 'Bravo to these ten people. They are either the strongest or the smartest or the luckiest. But forty more balloons are still left inside. Now what? I give you five more minutes and a twist. This time around, each one of you will go inside the room, pick a random balloon and give it to the person whom it belongs to.'

In sixty seconds, all forty were out of the room with their respective balloons.

The speaker then began, 'You gave them their balloon and you eventually found your own. The first time you tried to only think about your own balloon and created chaos. Only ten of you were successful. The second time, you thought about others; hence, each one of you was successful much quicker and together.'

Help someone and someone else will help you. Give people happiness and you will find your own happiness. It's the circle of life.

We have made life a race. We have completely stopped thinking about each other. Everyone is frantically looking for their individual success and hence, only a few of us, the strongest, the smartest or the luckiest, have it.

Therefore, let us smile, thank, apologise, share and be positive always. The sun's energy never reduces despite radiating round the clock. Let's be like the sun which always illuminates and energises everything around it and its absence darkens everything.

Let's be like a honeybee who selflessly collects nectar and pollen and shares the same, but is still never short of honey.

Let's look at giving from a much wider perspective and make sure that it's an endless flow from us to humanity and society.

12

Networking

Networking is more about 'farming' than it is about 'hunting'; it's about cultivating relationships.

—Ivan Misner

Today, networking has become a very important tool to grow and expand business across sectors, segments and locations. Social media and professional business network platforms like BNI and JBN have played a very important role in highlighting and popularising the power and effectiveness of networking. It started with an idea to help the businesses grow by creating a network of effective contacts and connections but has gone beyond that limited purpose to touching every point of our life, social as well as business.

The network of contacts we create is no less effective than Google in helping us to find solutions and answers to our problems and needs. Unlike Google, the solutions have a trust element attached to it as they come from a known reference.

Just as any brilliant person needs a team or group to assist in the journey, similarly we need a network of people who would support us without any direct quid pro by opening up so many closed doors effortlessly (the earlier chapter on 'sharing' was to throw light on the fact that it provides motivation and is one of the reasons behind networks being effective). As good as your Public Relations are, it's not possible to have direct access to all people we need to connect in life. If we need a reliable lawyer in X city, we need a connect in city X who can introduce us to a reliable lawyer in that city. Similarly, for an event in city Y, if we need a local Event manager, the same comes easy if we have an established network in city Y, which we can tap whenever needed.

In short, we can define networking as creating connections and relationships across different fields and platforms which we can access as and when needed. We never know when and where a need arises, hence, networks are created not necessarily with a defined objective but with a general purpose to meet and know people from different walks of life. We always learn and gain from people from varied backgrounds as everyone has something to add to our lives in a big or small way.

Many a times we err by focussing on networking with only powerful personalities but it has been seen more than once that a peon has proved to be more helpful than an apparently resourceful person. Needs vary and hence, networking needs to be wide and diverse. As we travel in our life journey, we meet many but the skill is to create a connection with all with a smile or helping hand so that the tentacles of our reach keep spreading wide and deep. Never underestimate or ignore anyone as the world is round and you never know when and where you will meet that person again.

We have seen our quiet and unnoticed school and college friends grow to become powerful and important people. However, our attitude has made us lose the connection with them that we rue later in life.

Networking is an ongoing process and just like a tree keeps spreading its roots and branches, we also need to keep growing our network through various mediums so that nothing is beyond us if we really want to reach somewhere.

Networking should not be mixed with friendship and close relationships. Those will always be limited and precious. However, we can still be connected with a much larger audience through social media, wishes on special occasions, warmth in the interface on different platforms and so on. It does not mean devoting special time to any individual but just doing enough to create a linkage that can be activated as and when wished. We may call it selfishness but it really isn't, as we will hardly ever need more than 0.5 per cent of our network and moreover, we also give back to our network. It's more like insurance coverage where relationships are developed for a rare probability of a specific need or purpose.

The later chapters talk about marketing and communication which are very important and instrumental in creating an effective network. The more colourful and bright our rainbow is, the more people will love to engage and connect with us.

13

Communication

Precision of communication is important, more important than ever, in our era of hair-trigger balances, when a false or misunderstood word may create as much disaster as a sudden thoughtless act.

—James Thurber

Most of us know that no communication is complete unless it is understood in the same context by the receiver as intended by the speaker.

The irony is that though we know the above, we still hardly try to ensure that the receiver grasps our communication as we want them to. In fact, we go one step forward and blame it on the receiver if he doesn't understand us and takes a different meaning.

There is no dearth of communication classes, speakers and books to tell us how to communicate effectively and clearly. However, very few people actually engage with them and even fewer actually adopt the learnings. So, does it mean, most feel that they are great communicators?

Situation and environment play a very important role in communication. However, the biggest challenge is to gauge the different types of people we engage with and modify our communication accordingly. Great speakers speak and engage with an audience with widely diversified mindsets, IQ and EQ levels. The content isn't necessarily great and different always but the delivery surely is. This is the power of communication.

Communication is much more than words. It's the tone, body language and environment which builds it up. However, very few think about synchronising all together. So many times, we are bewildered and confused as to what was wrong in what we said that annoyed the other person! We reassure ourselves that we are right by telling ourselves, 'I just said this' or 'I was so calm' or 'I was just being honest or nice'.

Unlike a courier package, which is delivered as sent, communication collects a lot on its way before being delivered and that may change the meaning and essence of the message.

Chapters on *Anekantvaad*, marketing, asking questions, etc. have covered the importance of communication and also indirectly given tips on how to be a good communicator.

However, considering the importance of the subject in our lives, I wanted to directly raise this question to you and highlight a few simple things which could raise the quality of communication.

This book which I have written is also nothing but communication. The success would depend on how it is received and understood by the reader or at least by my target audience.

One simple thing to always remember is: 'Know and understand your audience(s).'

You have to keep in mind their:

- Relationship with you—it's different depending on whether you are talking to your boss, employees, parents, children, wife or a group that is spending time and money to hear you
- Knowledge level
- Likes and dislikes
- Mood

- Temperament
- Receptiveness towards you and your current relationship with them
- The environment in which communication is being made

Try your best to put yourself in the other person's shoes and see things from their perspective. Always remember what we think and translate into words and actions may not get exactly retranslated in the same way to the other person. The stimulations and vibrations picked up by the recipient may convey a different meaning.

The same thing said to two different people at the same time may be comprehended differently. Similarly, the same thing said by two different people in the same tone may be understood differently by the same person.

We have seen many a times that the most knowledgeable teacher isn't the best and the favourite teacher of students. It is all because they cannot communicate their knowledge effectively.

Further, it is important to try and understand how effectively we have communicated. Many a times, we feel we have done a great job, but surprisingly, it can be just the opposite. This is a very dangerous situation as understanding a situation might be as distant as the North Pole and the South Pole.

Another important part of communication is to understand what the receiver understood or felt about what we conveyed to them. We first need to try to communicate as accurately as possible and then make our own report card. It's like both writing and evaluating the examination paper. We need to close the circle we initiated by starting a communication.

We are dependent on the receiver's communication skills, so obviously it is more difficult but we can pick up cues and signals from their reactions, words, tone, body language and so on.

As a speaker, I always love looking and speaking to those in the audience who keep nodding their heads and smiling as they keep telling me that I am correct and they are enjoying my talk. Similarly, if the majority of the crowd have started using their mobile phones, it's a message to pack up.

Furthermore, we should be able to communicate our understanding as a receiver to the sender. Communication isn't just about conveying but also understanding and receiving the correct meaning of a sender by going beyond words and picking up the right cues. Just as we hate to be misunderstood, so do others.

Hence, to be a good communicator, we need to:

- Ensure that the intent and meaning of our communication is well received by the intended recipient.
- Understand the real intent and meaning of what another person is conveying.
- Communicate back to the sender our understanding to provide him an opportunity to rework if there is an unintended gap or misunderstanding.

Do take a pause and analyse some of the recent conversations (or arguments) you have had. Ask yourself, was it the content that created disagreements or was it just a misunderstanding? Ask yourself, could I have done it better? If so, then how and resolve to make a better attempt next time or maybe even remedy the past situation by trying to convey the same thing in a better way.

14

Branding and Marketing

Branding gives you an exceptionally effective way to broadcast who you are to your target market quickly and efficiently.

—Rick Haskins

For students, marketing is a subject or a field of specialisation that teaches them to market products and services. For job seekers, it's a job opportunity and in business, it's the way to sell your products and services and achieve more revenue and profit.

However, I wanted to give this word a different perspective and show how important this word is in our lives. Many students ask me whether they should specialise in marketing or finance but I wonder, is marketing really an option in life or an integral part to succeed?

Marketing is something we start practising right from day one. It is needed in every walk of life, whether it is for attention from parents, school interview, making friends and so on. At every stage of life, we are knowingly or unknowingly marketing ourselves. We are trying to prove ourselves to someone or the other. Even between family and friends, we are marketing ourselves to get their attention, love and affection.

I know all this makes you sound like a product but the race to prove ourselves and to get attention and appreciation is also a form of marketing. Some call it PR (public relations) but it is a form of marketing only. We are projecting ourselves so that people like and love our company. Don't we dress up to look good at a party so that we are noticed and appreciated? Isn't this like packaging a product to make it more marketable?

In a marriage, don't we match the attributes of each and check compatibility just like we do while buying a product by matching it with our needs and requirements? When we go on a date, don't we try to present ourselves so that the other person likes us and wants to go out with us again?

Even Einstein would not have been what he was if he didn't market/communicate his inventions to the world and convince it of its truth and applicability. We always say that a great idea needs to be executed and communicated to complete the circle. Successful people are not those who thought of innovative and new things but those who were able to take it to the world and change the lives of people.

Last but not least, what about all the posts we share on social media like Facebook? Is it just sharing ourselves with our closed ones or something more than that?

If by now, you have accepted that marketing is an integral part of our lives, let us see how we can market ourselves better or can we do without marketing ourselves?

Marketing is an awkward and crude word to use for oneself but here I just wanted to be as blunt and direct as possible. More important than the word is the real essence and meaning.

In a way, everything written in this book would make you a better marketer but let's try to get a bit more specific and practical.

Marketing is a very vast field and not even multiple books can cover the complete subject. Today we are in a dynamic world where the environment is changing faster than we realise. Rather than change, disruption is the norm. Even before we learn, things become obsolete. Hence, I don't feel that situation-based learning will help beyond a point.

However, I would leave some pointers which will surely make you more likeable, fancied and a better company for the world around you. These are very simple things but ask yourself, how many do you practice?

Just like products, we also develop identities that may also be called branding. Our real brand is what people say and think about us in our absence and the compliments and praises dished out to us. More importantly, do remember that if we don't build the 'Brand You', someone else may brand you with the wrong label.

Marketing yourself can also be called interpersonal skills, public relations and so on, but I feel all are subsets of marketing and projecting ourselves. We say many a times that good interpersonal skills are important to be a successful marketer but it doesn't mean every such person will be the best in marketing.

Some simple marketing tips for the consideration of all:

- Smile and be cheerful
- Put yourself in others' position and understand their perspectives
- Be confident and believe in yourself—that we are better than most around us
- Think differently and question the obvious or in other words, be interesting
- Believe in sharing and giving
- Be flexible and adaptable

The list can go on and on but it is better to have a small doable list and start doing rather than just believing and agreeing.

15

Expectations

When you stop expecting people to be perfect,
you can like them for who they are.
—Donald Miller

Life is never complete unless we have inner peace and harmony. We may gather many accolades in life. However, the quality of relationships we have around us plays a very key role in our life.

We normally relate happiness and peace to health and wealth but I think the mind and heart are most disturbed by our relationships with fellow human beings. No one is perfect in this world. We all agree to the same but still expect that others should be perfect despite our imperfections. We may not be able to see others from multiple angles but we expect to be completely understood.

It is unfortunate but true that expectations play a very important role in our life. It may be for events, results, behaviour and performances but in all cases, the deviation from our expectations is one of the biggest sources of disturbance in our life. We are not so much disturbed by reality as much as we are from the deviation of the same from our expectations.

Expectations can be both internal and external but both can be equally damaging in their own way.

Let's say, we expected our boss to shout at us but he just reprimands us; we are pleasantly surprised. However, if we expected him not to be angry, then his mild irritation also disturbs us.

If we expected to get 85 per cent marks and received 90 per cent, we are elated but if we expected 95 per cent, then even with 94 per cent we are disappointed.

This gets more serious when we enter the realm of relationships. Most breakups and heartbreaks happen when our expectations get shattered due to contrarian behaviour. Friendships and relationships break up just because of expectation variance between two people and their inability to handle the same. It's important to learn to 'agree to disagree' rather than expecting complete agreement in relationships. Imperfections are at times more beautiful than perfection.

This will, of course, raise a simple question in our minds: 'Are expectations bad? Should we never have one?' The answer is equally simple. Expectations are not bad. They are very natural and cannot be stopped as they are an integral part of our life. They also, in a way, propel us to move forward and work harder to achieve our goals. As someone said, if we won't have expectations from our near and dear ones, then from whom should we have them?

We have expectations from others but we expect others not to expect from us. We need to understand that we should first give rather than expect.

The critical thing is how we handle the deviation from our expectations. Can we accept that all expectations in life can never be fulfilled? Some will be met and many will be not. Is it possible to develop that level of maturity to understand and appreciate the failures?

Expectations can really strangulate your life and burn you from the inside if we don't, beyond a point, let them go and accept things as they are.

Expectations are never-ending and they keep growing to a level that is practically impossible to meet. Hence, whether it is from us or others, there will always be a breaking point.

The ones who break due to their own failures are still easy to understand as we can benchmark ourselves relatively easily. However, the ones who break due to others' performance or behaviour are really the difficult ones.

The other person, most of the time, doesn't even know or understand the expectations that we have from them. Hence, one doesn't even realise that one is the cause of our expectations breaking and the ensuing disappointment and pain that builds inside us. There is a complete disconnection which aggravates the situation due to the behaviour emanating for this disconnection.

Let's learn to accept the fact that all our expectations will not be met. Let's accept that everyone has their own yardstick and understanding which doesn't necessarily have to match with ours. We all are individuals and unique in our own way. We must respect others to gain their respect. Let's expect but not build true relationships on expectations from others, rather, let's build them on our own expectations from ourselves.

Internally, let's allow expectations to rise from our dreams and motivate us forward. However, as discussed earlier in the book, we must understand the elasticity of the rubber band that is life and know its breaking level. Do not expect miracles from life but learn to work to achieve your dreams and expectations by karma.

The balance of life needs to be maintained while we forge ahead in this ruthless and competitive life. A chariot with a broken wheel cannot get too far.

Trust is an important counter to expectations. If we trust ourselves and people around us, we shall not blame anyone for not living up to our expectations. Trust ensures that we accept the same as incidental and coincidence, and hence, there is no ill feeling created by assuming the other's behaviour as intentional, which breaks our expectations.

If we recollect, I am sure we shall find many incidents where we unintentionally hurt people, but they feel it is done purposefully. We normally feel we know more than the people around us but when it comes to expectations, we feel they should have known it all.

I am writing this book with a lot of heart and expectations but it may just fall flat and disappoint me. I will need to redirect my energies in another direction and not allow them to dissipate by a failure.

We all have been blessed with moments where we have got more than expected in life. While we have enjoyed them fully with gratefulness, we should also be ready to bear disappointment.

Expect, but don't allow it to break us or our relationships.

Even Lord Krishna said: 'Keep doing your karma without expectation of reward, God will ensure you are suitably rewarded at the opportune time.'

16

Best Versus Right

The best thing isn't always the RIGHT thing,
but the right thing is always the BEST thing.
—Anonymous

It's very normal for all of us to want the best of everything in life. Since we start consciously thinking for ourselves, we start wanting the best things and even the second best does not satisfy us. Out of compulsion we accept inferior things but our heart still yearns for the best and hence, there is a sense of emptiness that taints our whole life. The feeling of contentment, satisfaction and happiness is rarely felt and enjoyed by us in its purest form. However, from birth till when we reach this yearning stage, we feel the above things in the purest form because we don't know what is best but we surely know what is right for us. The attainment of what is right for us gives us bliss and happiness.

However, if we delve deep into what we want, the real happiness and satisfaction are in getting what is right for us and what is necessarily the best around us. And finally, what is right for us becomes the best for us though it may not be the best in the eyes of the world around us.

I will like to share some instances for you to ponder over:

- Do we want to hire the best or the right person for our job description? If the job doesn't give satisfaction to the employee, the chances of his continuity are remote and we waste resources training them for a job role that never suited them. There are jobs that can be suitably done with training by a class-eight-pass employee, then why hire a graduate?
- Is marrying the most popular and beautiful actress of our time the right thing for us to do? Or will we be happy marrying someone we are compatible with?

- Is a limousine the right car for us to travel on a busy road where parking is a nightmare? Or will a small car or two-wheeler be a better option?
- Are the clothes of a top designer the right attire for us when we go to the office?
- Is an IIT admission the right thing for a student with artistic instincts, skill and temperament?

We can ask ourselves the question in innumerable situations and we shall find that the right thing for us isn't necessarily the best thing around us. Our situation, our position, our attitude, our comfort zone and our choices will determine what is the right thing for us and that right will ultimately be the best for us. All the above instances show the best isn't necessarily the right thing for us.

Hence, we don't need to run behind what we feel is the best thing around and get depressed when we can't achieve or own it. We need to see what is right for us and pursue that quietly while the world around us is crazily spending their resources and energy to attain the very best and being caught in a never-ending pursuit.

Let's start redefining our goals and objectives as to what is right for us. Let's not allow the environment and people around us to decide our course of action. We should be our own masters and have the conviction to decide for ourselves.

Many years back, while attending a reunion in IIMA, I had a chance to interact with the current batch of students. It was a tough year for placement after the Lehman crisis and the students were concerned and sought help from alumni for placement. I said that even if I get an IIM student free of cost, I will not hire them. Everyone looked at me, surprised. The fact was that it would take me months of training to make them worthy to contribute positively and I was sure that at the first opportunity they would leave my mid-sized company and move on. The same happened with UCO Bank who eventually got eight IIM graduates that year but could not retain anyone for any significant period of time.

Both employer and employee need to find their right fit and not just go for the best option available.

It's always more graceful to wear a good-fitting shirt rather than an expensive shirt which is ill-fitting.

Despite being from the textile industry, I have refrained from talking much about it. However, I will like to share one example to push this point. In knitted fabric used in T-shirts, we talk about grams per sq. metre (gsm) to denote the thickness of the fabric. Mostly when we have a specification of 150 gsm fabric, our production team, to be on the safer side, plans for 155 gsm so that the product doesn't get rejected, though they take the plea that we want to give the best. This small thing increases the cost by 3 per cent which could have been saved if we had just stuck to giving the right product (this, of course, means more care and attention as best provides buffer and comfort). In life, many a times, we just go for the best to reduce the risk and create a buffer/comfort for ourselves; which is missing when we endeavour to be 'just right'. As they say, there are no free lunches. This delta of best and right also has a cost.

We all are like seeds with a potential to grow into a full-fledged tree. We shall be different trees but we all have a purpose and utility. Different seeds need different additives to grow; abundant sunlight and water do not necessarily lead to the best growth of a seed. We need to add the right additives to every seed to make it grow to its full potential.

Hope this simple thought will push us to have a happier and peaceful life with less despair and more satisfaction. *Best* is relative and moving, hence, difficult to attain; but *right* is easier to ascertain and reach.

17

Who Are We?

Everybody is a genius. But if you judge a fish by its ability to climb a tree, it will live its whole life believing that it is stupid.

—Albert Einstein

This question sounds simple but is actually very complex and difficult. We are so busy in analysing and knowing the people around us that we actually forget about ourselves. Even someone like Hanumanji needed to be reminded of his inner strengths and capabilities and gain the confidence for doing things.

We always feel—who can know ourselves better than us? However, we are proven wrong more than once. We normally err by a margin and hence end up grossly under or overestimating ourselves.

We are a bundle of so many chemicals, neurons, atoms and genes that its extraordinarily difficult to understand ourselves—emotions, preferences, tastes, capabilities and choices. It's also not a one-time process as we keep evolving over time and new combinations evolve in us to create new potentials and capabilities. 1+1 sometimes may make an 11 instead of 2 and make us emerge as a different force. We are so many times amazed to see people emerge and become dominant forces in life, which is totally unexpected and unimaginable. I am sure if we all look back at our school and college friends and try to map them as per our estimations, we shall see more than 10 per cent shocking us and another 20–30 per cent surprising us.

I myself am a living example of having transformed myself from my school days into what I am today. My school friends would never have imagined that a quiet and shy boy would emerge so strongly in life. I myself never imagined that I would change myself so much and give a different direction to my life. I have never even believed I had it in me to do what all I have done and plan to do ahead. I have surprised myself multiple times in life, but still, I am discovering and learning more about myself.

It's utmost important to stretch and push ourselves, to check out the real potential and capability of ourselves. We are like an elastic and need to be pulled to get stretched. How much stretchability we have can only be known by pulling ourselves and testing the same. Different attributes and capabilities inside us will have varying potentials which we need to discover. I just plead to all, let's not decide about ourselves without knowing or trying. Our feelings about ourselves are not necessarily the final word, not even for those who have lived their life. People surprise themselves at all ages, so do not be disheartened. We never know when the jigsaw puzzle inside us gets set and what looks like a hopeless position becomes an insurmountable power.

Don't allow someone else to tell you that you cannot do something. Most of them hardly know you enough to pass a final verdict. Who can know you better than yourself? So you decide your chances, limits and probabilities and chart your course of action. It's not wrong to listen to others but it's wrong to allow them to decide for you.

We all are aware of the saying that failures are pillars of success. It's basically the evolution of a person as he learns in his life journey which makes him gather himself together to finally succeed.

I agree there are many things in the world which we cannot possibly do despite conviction and confidence. However, there are still so many things that can be done by us which sound or seem impossible. The energy inside us is so immense and powerful that if nurtured and pushed, it can become like a cyclone that can sweep us off our feet and land us in a totally different orbit.

As discussed earlier, we are in the world of volatility and disruption, and hence, time is no bar to success and achievement. I have seen more than one person who did not have the guts to even stand in front of the public, delivering fantastic speeches when pushed and empowered to do so. It's just not about where we reach; it's about whether we are moving forward or not.

Many need mentors and guides to be inspired, motivated and pushed. However, I request everyone to not be a 'Hanumanji' who lacks confidence in himself and needs someone else to understand him. Every human being is unique; we all have unimaginable powers in us. We just need to believe in ourselves and embark on our life journey to achieve our goals and fulfil our dreams.

One simple exercise which I use whenever I want to push myself, is to take a deep breath and steel myself with a thought. Let me give it my best shot and what's the worst that I can lose from this effort? In most cases, the negatives are trivial in front of the positives.

Maybe you cannot be a Lata Mangeshkar or Usain Bolt or Sachin Tendulkar but there are surely many things and avenues where you can be a leader. We all have our own choices, preferences and dreams. Let's just pursue them and trust ourselves. As they say, doing nothing leads one nowhere. However, doing something will either give you success or learnings. You can never be a loser by making a positive effort.

Some may be thinking, when finally will we know our ourselves completely and be able to confidently say 'Who are we?' I guess probably never, and it really doesn't matter. However, remember the fun is in moving upwards from 20 per cent to

90 per cent rather than reaching 100 per cent. So keep pushing, learning and enjoying the journey and I am 100 per cent sure you will surprise yourself with your attainments and achievements.

Another point to ponder is 'what are we good at?' and 'what do we enjoy doing?' It may seem obvious that they both would be same but surprisingly it's not necessary and in fact, in most cases, they are different things. We may be good at mathematics but may enjoy singing. We typically end up making a career of what we are good at and make a hobby of what we enjoy. However, it's very much possible to find overlaps and a sweet spot so we enjoy our work by leveraging our skills and strengths. For example, if you enjoy sports but are not good enough to be a professional, you can start a business related to sports equipment or management.

I would like to share a second-standard (in school) story of mine where I had come to India as my parents shifted from England to India (my father was a doctor who studied in England and I was born there). I struggled badly with the Indian education system and did the impossible—failing in all subjects and just aggregating 11 per cent marks. The class teacher was confident that I would need to repeat the class. However, the unbelievable happened and within six months, I turned the corner decisively and not only passed in all subjects but attained 80 per cent marks. This journey of 11 per cent to 80 per cent in just six months showed that efforts and determination could make you scale higher than dreams and imaginations. I value this report card more than those where I have consistently topped.

It's just not about where you are but also about where you can go. The past should be learnt and not dragged. We need to keep pushing and moving to understand and learn about ourselves as we travel down our life journey. It's a continuous discovery of our immense and deep powers which we have been endowed with.

18

Create Our Rainbow

It takes sunshine and rain to make a rainbow. There would be no rainbows without sunshine and rain.
—Roy T. Bennett

Just as we cannot pull at an elastic band beyond a certain point, we need to understand that we all have our limitations. Everyone can't become Carl Lewis but, again, even Carl Lewis can be worse than us in many things. We need to explore and find our inner strengths and then leverage them to take ourselves to the next orbit.

Failing in mathematics isn't the end of the world; you still can be a world-class artist, designer, historian, speaker and so on.

We don't need to copy or ape anyone in the world; we are human beings and are individuals.

We are 'we' and should be proud of ourselves. We just need to understand and appreciate ourselves and stretch our capabilities and strengths in the right direction.

Most of us live our lives under the burden of meeting others' expectations, creating an image in the eyes of others, worrying what others think or feel about us and so on. We stifle ourselves under these superficial pressures and the butterfly of our life gets suppressed in the cocoon of external pressures, which, if looked objectively, are meaningless in more than one way.

There are certain basic norms of society and life which we need to follow, that is, we should not hurt others, become a nuisance to the public, shy away from the responsibilities we have accepted or are obligated to fulfil, etc., but that's where it should end. For example, if we do not want to bring up children and be responsible for their growth and development, it's fine, but we should then not plan and have children in our life.

We have the right to choose our seven colours and build our life rainbow. As discussed in the first chapter, truth and right are perceptions that will vary from person to person. So let's not burden ourselves or others within a spectrum which one doesn't enjoy or find comfort in.

Our choices are not always obvious and they are prone to change as we gain exposure, experience and knowledge. We need to give ourselves time to understand ourselves and the world. There is always a gestation period before a caterpillar becomes a butterfly; so is the case with humans. We all have the right to take corrective action and change the course of life, so don't be afraid of mistakes or failures as they are an essential part of life.

Think and contemplate over things, particularly those involving long-term commitments and responsibilities. Never rush, especially when your decisions affect others and always value both mind and heart in choosing your colours of life.

However, many often, life does not give us choices; we just have one path to follow. At times in life, we have to take the plunge and then make the best of it. Once taken, it is better to be positive and try to carve out your comfort zone from the given set of circumstances rather than brooding about it.

Just as many other things in this book, it is easier said than done. But remember, we have nothing to lose, so why not give it a try? The rose isn't the only beautiful flower in this world; there are many other flowers which are equally beautiful and soothing. A yellow rose is preferred over a red rose when we meet a friend; so everything has its own purpose in life. And you also do have your purpose which you need to just find and recognise.

Life is a bouquet of experiences and actions. Hence, enjoy all facets of life, that is, all colours—some more, some less. Rather than regretting, it is better to experience and live the different colours and create your own rainbow. Some colours will be lighter and some darker, but the overall rainbow created will still be beautiful as seen from the horizon of life.

A rainbow is nothing but a splitting of light into multiple colours. Similarly, we are sources of energy and light that will get refracted, reflected and dispersed in our life journey to create a beautiful rainbow. We need to feel and recognise *our inner light* and project the same in our wonderful life.

Let's create our own rainbow with our unique colours.

19

Our Obituary

Our goals can only be reached through a vehicle of a plan, in which we must fervently believe, and upon which we must vigorously act. There is no other route to success.

—Pablo Picasso

Do not get alarmed by the chapter heading. An obituary is the last text written about a person on death which summarises his or her life journey. The idea behind this chapter is to shake us up and ring a wake-up call in our life. No one wants to die with a feeling of vacuum and unfulfillment; we all desire to die with a smile of satisfaction and contentment. There is, of course, no end to one's desires and dreams. However, there are still things one wants to do and achieve in a lifetime.

In the earlier chapters, we have spoken of knowing ourselves and creating our life rainbow. I just wanted to take it one step deeper by ending the book with this thought and appeal to all. We can never reach anywhere if we don't know the desired destination. It is, however, also true that many a times the journey is more beautiful and interesting than the ultimate goal. However, we still need to know where we want to go. The destination may keep changing but still, it's the light which motivates us to keep moving ahead.

Many of us, unfortunately, don't know what we want from life and where we want to go. This confusion stymies us and we sort of pause in life by just going round and round. If people really look at their lives, many will see that they are not going anywhere really, they are just living on as they were born to live. Even when they are young, they don't wake up with any excitement whereas, a person like Warren Buffet is still excited at the age of eighty-eight. It's not just about the age, it's also about mindset. We also cannot blame anyone as, when they don't know where they have to or want to go, how can they move on?

I was not sure about what the book cover should be and what I would really write but because I wanted to do this, I did it. I prepared and wrote my CAT examination because I have wanted to do my MBA from IIM Ahmedabad since the eighth standard. There was a goal in front of me and I covered many milestones and made many decisions to reach there. I did Cost Accountancy to be more qualified than my peers when I went for an IIMA interview. However, that turned out to be my first major outstanding milestone in life.

It is not necessary that we all have to have earth-shattering goals; it's just that we need to have some purpose, excitement and something to achieve. In an interview when asked, 'Where do you see yourself after ten years?', someone said, 'Happily married with two lovely children and a nice home.' It was not about career achievements but he still got hired.

Finally coming to the chapter heading, where does the word 'obituary' fit in? This is really a post-mortem of our life and not about the goals or destination. However, here also, we can view the thing differently and see positivity. We can write our own obituary in advance, the way we want to be remembered by the world when we go. This can act as a 'life plan' or a 'vision document' and help us decide what the major things are that we want to achieve in life and then we can work towards them. It is said that in this changing world, it is difficult to plan things but there are still broader things which can be planned like, 'I want to be instrumental in creating an impact on society' or 'I want to be a leader in whatever business I do' or 'I want to travel to a hundred countries' and so on.

Once a group of friends decided to give purpose and direction to their lives. They decided to write their obituary assuming they would die after four years. This gave them a list of the most important things in their lives and a time-bound mission to work on in the next four years.

I am sure at least in our subconsciousness, we all have dreams. Let's put them down on paper and then embark on the journey. It's never too late in life to change track and move ahead. The past should only teach us, not demotivate us. We attend various condolence and funeral programs where we are told about the demised person and I am sure you see a difference between achievers and those who just lived. Just think about how you want to be remembered and spoken about.

Let's write our own obituary and ensure it makes us and our family proud. The legacies we leave are as important as the genes we give to our children. Even today, despite seventeen years of his passing, I enjoy the goodwill of my father and still meet the people who remember him fondly for his smile and treating many patients as a surgeon. Everything dies but impactful deeds live on and that's why a subject like history exists.

We are all stories in the end; let's just make it a good one.

Conclusion

Does everything in life have to be concluded? Do all questions in life have to be answered? Do we always need to reach a conclusion or solution? Is there really an end to things in life?

These are the questions which come to me as I write this ending note. I am not sure if there needs to be a conclusion but still, for the sake of completeness and to summarise, I sign off with this chapter.

The thoughts and issues shared can never be adopted in totality to create a perfect world. Every edge cannot be rounded and smoothened; some have to be sharp and angled.

I thank you for being patient to have read through (at least I hope you have) and I would just like to reiterate some key takeaways. This sharing is not meant to be a one-time read, but food for thought and contemplation. I don't want this to be like a motivational speech which we all agree with but hardly ever practise. I have tried to keep the points very simple, focussed, understandable and easy to practise.

Most of the thoughts shared may seem to be more relevant to a context, but trust me, most of them can be applied in various aspects of our life. The context may not be universal but the applicability is.

You may agree fully or partially but do think about these points during your wonderful life journey:

- There are different perspectives on things; let us try to understand the viewpoint of others too.
- Change is obvious but to stand out, you need to disrupt the norm.
- Think differently and try to practise your ideas differently.
- Be a professional.
- Time is not just hours but the work you do in it.
- Never fear to ask questions.
- Learning never stops.
- Problems are the best teacher; you cannot succeed without them.

- Do what's possible rather than worrying about things that are not in our control.
- Hope should always be combined with directed action.
- At least share your infinite resources.
- Power of networking.
- Communication is never complete until understood in the right sense.
- Marketing is not a choice but a part of life.
- Expectations are good if understood and controlled.
- The best isn't always right for you.
- Understand yourself.
- Create your own rainbow.
- Dream and fulfil your wishes.

These are small, simple and obvious things. They are as simple and common as salt. However, without that pinch of salt, a dish is never complete. Similarly, the recipe of life is never complete without these basic and common things in life.

The list of positive ingredients needed for life is endless; I have just highlighted a few. There are so many, like, hard work, integrity, discipline, smartness, positivity, etc., which are equally or more important in life.

I wish everyone a great, exciting and fantastic journey. Let's live life rather than just pass it.

And whenever the journey is complete, may we leave a beautiful rainbow over the horizon for others to see, enjoy and admire.

I hope, like a honeybee who seeks nectar ignoring the negatives in the surroundings, you have also found some nectar in this book to sweeten the lives of everyone around you. Please don't keep it just with you but share it with people and let it multiply. Let us desist from being like flies who seek dirt and trash ignoring the beautiful surroundings.

Always hear what others are saying but do what you feel is right. As they say, '*Suno sabki, per karo apni*.'

About the Author

Sanjay K. Jain is a double gold medallist from IIM Ahmedabad, apart from being a rank-holder cost accountant and rank-holder commerce graduate. He is also a qualified company secretary.

He has had the privilege of working with top investment bankers and running his own finance company before joining TT Limited. Having headed three national-level textile associations, he is also involved in policymaking at Centre and state levels and is also actively involved in various social projects spanning health and education. He has been an active mentor for students, social and business start-ups in countries such as India, Kenya, Australia and the USA. He is a member of social institutions like Lions, Jain International Trade Organisation

(JITO), Terapanth Professional Forum (TPF) and Bharatiya Jain Sanghatana (BJS).

Sanjay is a recipient of numerous awards—the Udyog Ratna, Outstanding Businessman and Industrialist Award, Asia Pacific Entrepreneurship Award, BW GOPIO Global Business Award, ET Business Leader Award and CEO with HR Orientation Award.

A prolific speaker, Sanjay has written many articles and been featured in magazines such as *Business India*, *Marwar India* and *Insight*. He believes in sharing his knowledge which has motivated him to start BiznessClinic, a unique social project to mentor MSMEs/start-ups.

This is his first book and he can be contacted at pinchofsalt0007@gmail.com